LEARN TO DRAW

Disney

FROZEN

Illustrated by The Disney Storybook Artists

Walter Foster
Jr.

Published by Walter Foster Jr.,
an imprint of Quarto Publishing Group USA Inc.
6 Orchard Road, Suite 100, Lake Forest, CA 92630

Printed in China

5 7 9 10 8 6 4

Table of Contents

Tools & Materials

You only need a few art supplies to create all of your favorite characters from *Frozen*. Start with a drawing pencil, and have a pencil sharpener and an eraser nearby. When you've finished drawing, you can add color with felt-tip markers, colored pencils, watercolors, or acrylic paint. The choice is yours!

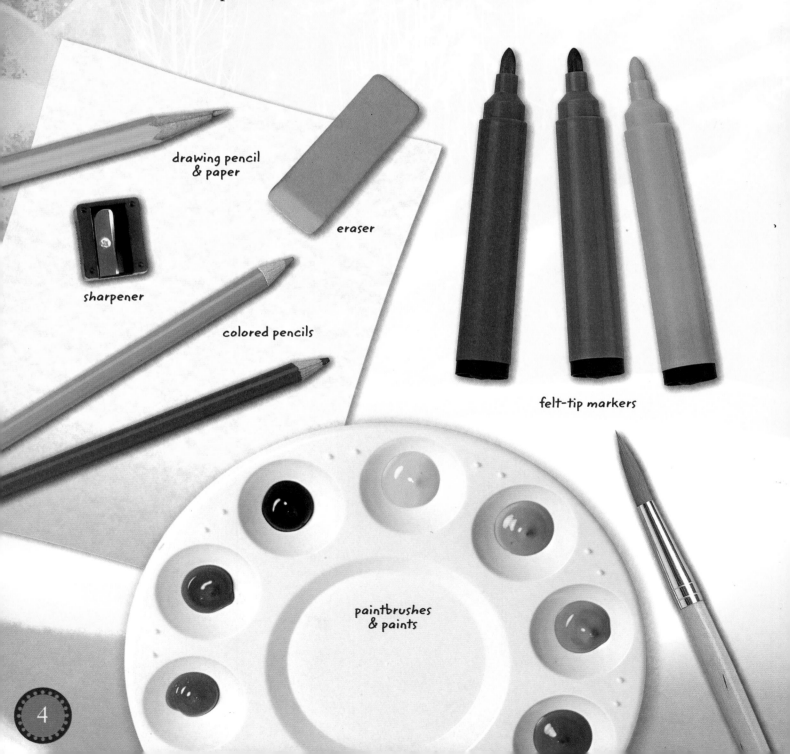

drawing pencil & paper

eraser

sharpener

colored pencils

felt-tip markers

paintbrushes & paints

How to Use This Book

In this book you'll learn to draw your favorite characters in just a few simple steps. You'll also get lots of helpful tips from Disney artists that will guide you through the drawing process. With a little practice, you'll soon be creating new drawings of your own!

First draw the basic shapes, using light lines that are easy to erase.

Each new step is shown in blue, so you know what to draw next.

Follow the blue lines to draw the details.

Now darken the lines you want to keep, and erase the rest.

Use some of Elsa's magic (or crayons and markers) to add color to your drawing!

The Story of
FROZEN

Anna and Elsa are royal sisters, growing up in the faraway northern kingdom of Arendelle. As young girls, the princesses are close, and Elsa shares a secret with her little sister—she has the magical ability to create ice and snow. But when Anna is accidentally injured, Elsa realizes that her powers can also be dangerous. Afraid for both girls, the king and queen decide to limit Elsa's contact with the outside world. Ruled by the deep fear that she might hurt others, Elsa spends most of her time alone trying to hide her secret by controlling her emotions.

As the years pass, Anna runs happily around the castle but feels lonely without her sister, who avoids her at every turn. She has no idea that Elsa, behind closed doors, misses her too, and struggles every day to control her powers. When the king and queen are lost at sea, Elsa is next in line to become queen. For coronation day, the castle gates are opened for the first time in years. While Anna revels in the excitement of seeing new faces—and secretly hopes to find love—Elsa just hopes to keep her powers concealed.

The day of the coronation, Anna meets a visiting prince named Hans, and the two immediately fall in love. When Anna and Hans announce their engagement, Elsa scoffs at the idea. The sisters argue, and as Elsa's emotions get the best of her, a blast of ice covers the ballroom. Everyone is stunned.

Worried that she'll hurt someone, Elsa panics and flees the kingdom. Her emotions churn as she runs up a nearby mountain—but she starts to feel relieved too. Feeling free, with no one to worry about, she experiments with her magic and gives herself a stunning new look. Meanwhile, down in Arendelle, Anna assures the people she will find Elsa and embarks on a journey to persuade her sister, the queen, to come home.

Anna runs into one obstacle after another and eventually meets an ice-covered mountain man named Kristoff, who is traveling with his reindeer, Sven. Anna hires Kristoff to take her up the mountain to find Elsa. Along the way, they meet a cheerful little snowman named Olaf, who agrees to lead them to Elsa. Olaf's happy to help bring back warm weather because, contrary to all logic, he loves the idea of summer.

When the group finally arrives at the glittering ice palace high on the mountain, Elsa is surprised and worried to see her sister, admitting she doesn't know how to reverse the curse. She insists Anna leave and has trouble controlling her emotions when Anna refuses—a blast of ice emanates from her body and strikes Anna in the chest. Elsa creates a gigantic snowman named Marshmallow to carry Anna and Kristoff off the mountain. They flee in panic, escaping over the edge of a cliff.

Once they're safe, Kristoff sees that Anna's hair is turning white and she's freezing cold. He takes her to the realm of the trolls, known to be magical healers. The trolls consider Kristoff, an orphan, to be like an adopted son. But sadly, they cannot help Anna—a wise old troll named Grand Pabbie explains, "Only an act of true love can thaw a frozen heart."

As Anna continues to freeze, Kristoff rushes her back to Arendelle, convinced that a kiss from Hans will save her. But Hans reveals a cruel side that Anna didn't see before. He tells her he has captured and imprisoned Elsa and plans to take over the kingdom. Hans locks Anna alone in the library. Olaf unlocks the door with his nose and builds a fire to help warm Anna. He tells her that Kristoff loves her, and the two venture outside into the blinding snow to try to find him.

Meanwhile, Elsa's emotions overwhelm her and she is able to break out of her cell. She makes it to the frozen fjord, but Hans confronts her and tells her that Anna is dead. Elsa collapses to the ice, heartbroken; her worst fear has come true. As grief overwhelms her, the howling storm suddenly stops—the winds go silent and the snow is suspended in midair.

Suddenly everything on the fjord is visible. Anna turns and sees Kristoff, but not far away,

she also notices Elsa kneeling on the ice. For a moment, she looks at Kristoff, knowing if she doesn't reach him now she will freeze completely. She makes her choice—and throws herself in front of her sister just as Hans swings his sword. The sword breaks on Anna's fingertips as her body turns to ice. Realizing that Anna has just given her life to save her, Elsa begins weeping and embraces Anna's icy form. But then…Anna starts to melt. The spell has been broken! Anna displayed an act of true love when she sacrificed herself for her sister. The sisters hug and finally understand how much they love each other.

Elsa realizes that love—stronger than fear—is the solution to the curse. At last, she is able to bring summer back to Arendelle. The townspeople love their queen— and her powers, too! Elsa tells Anna she wants the castle gates to always stay open. Anna and Elsa are finally reunited, best friends and loyal sisters, in both snow and summer.

ANNA & ELSA
as Children

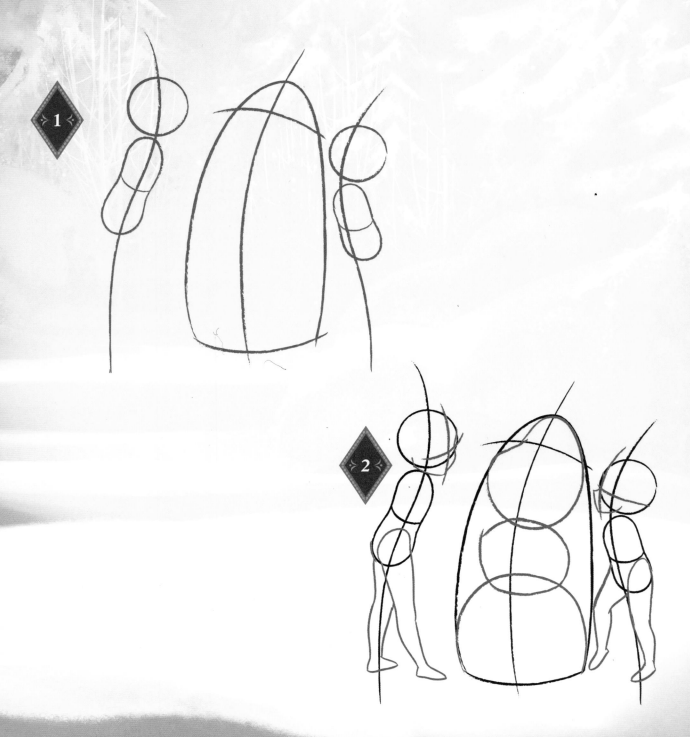

3

Elsa as a child is 4 heads tall

Anna as a child is 3 ½ heads tall

4

ANNA

Anna is optimistic and outgoing—a free spirit through and through. She always sees the best in everyone, and she longs to rekindle the love and friendship that she and Elsa once shared as children. After many lonely years spent cooped up in the palace, Anna dreams of finding adventure and love outside the gates, but she comes to realize that true love already exists in the most unexpected of places.

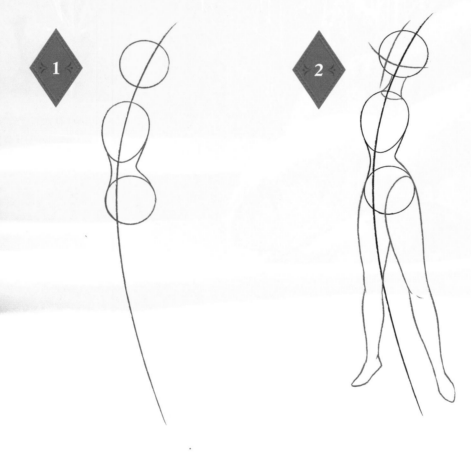

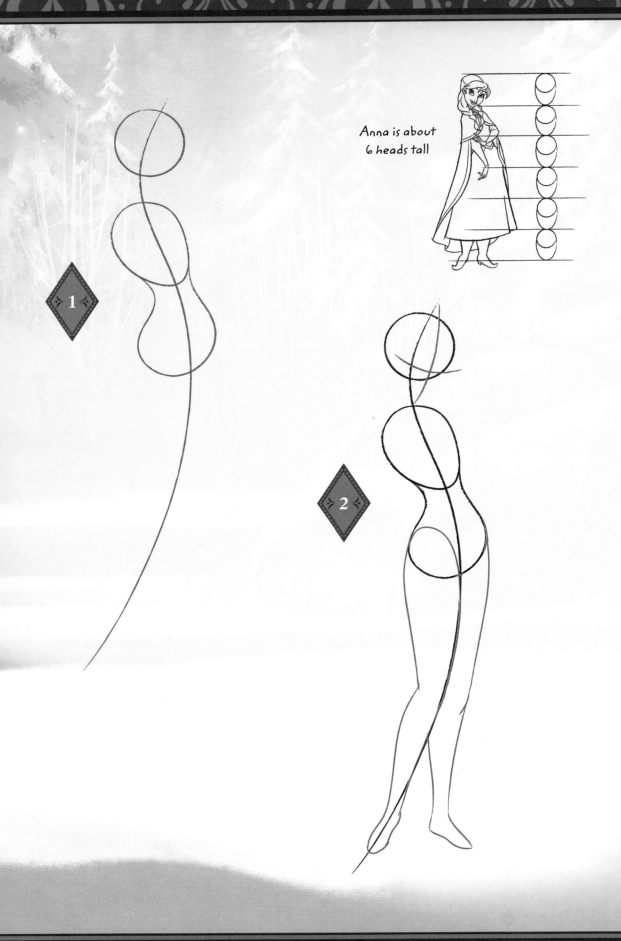

Anna is about
6 heads tall

1

2

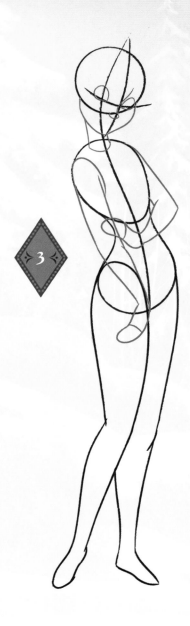

Top of Anna's eye
has a sharp angle

Bottom of eye
has rounder curve

5

YES

NO

Lines are sharp and angular, not rounded and soft

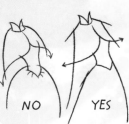
NO   YES

6

Anna's hands and fingers are sharp and thin, not soft and curvy

YES

NO

7

ELSA

Elsa is the perfect heir to the throne of Arendelle. Regal, graceful, and trustworthy, she is everything a queen should be. But Elsa hides a deep secret—she has the magical ability to create ice and snow. Elsa keeps herself locked away to protect others, but she must learn to trust her friends and let go of her fear; only then can she truly embrace her powers.

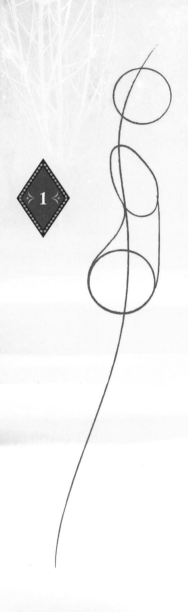

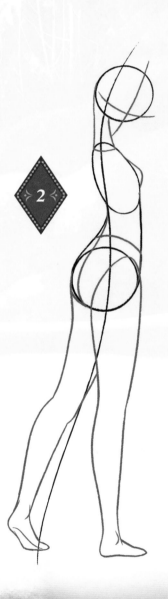

7

Elsa is about
6 ⅓ heads tall

◈ 3 ◈

◈ 4 ◈

Oval nose is horizontal, not angled

NO   YES

Eyes tilt up slightly

Top lip has a "dimple" in the middle

Upper lip is thinner than the lower lip

7

OLAF

Olaf is a curious and trusting snowman with a big heart. No bones about it,
Olaf is all about embracing life to its fullest! From warm hugs to summertime daydreams,
Olaf is filled with optimism and happiness. He always sees the bright side of any situation
and tries to help out whenever he can—even though it often gets him into trouble.
Although he's always loved the idea of summer and all things hot,
what he really wants is to be included as part of a family.

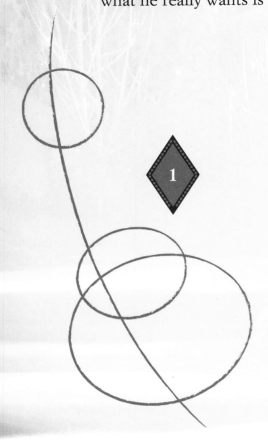

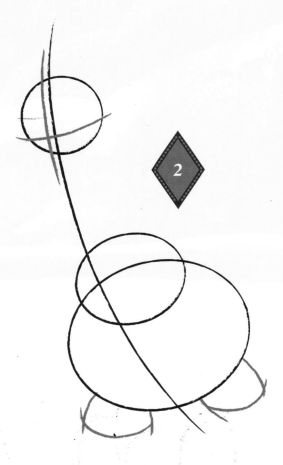

3

4

Olaf's body shapes are
slightly angular, not simple ovals

YES   NO

Don't Draw
your own

NO   YES

Olaf's hairs are irregular

5

6

Eyes are round and don't touch each other

NO   YES

Eyebrows are thick and full

7

Olaf's arms are sturdy twigs

YES

not soft and flexible

NO

KRISTOFF

Kristoff is an independent mountain man with a failing ice business. A little rough around the edges, he lives by his own rules and has a hard time trusting others. His only friend and companion is Sven, a clumsy yet endearing reindeer with whom he shares his deepest thoughts and feelings. Kristoff says that he prefers to be alone, but deep down he wants to find someone who knows and accepts him for exactly who he is.

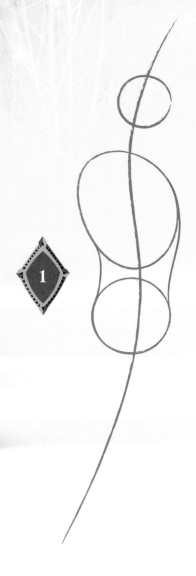

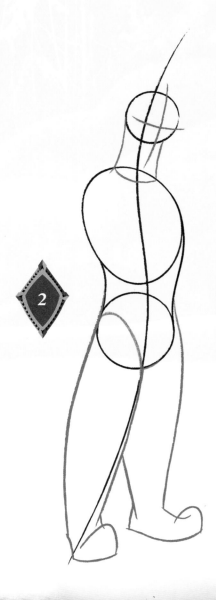

Kristoff is 6 heads tall

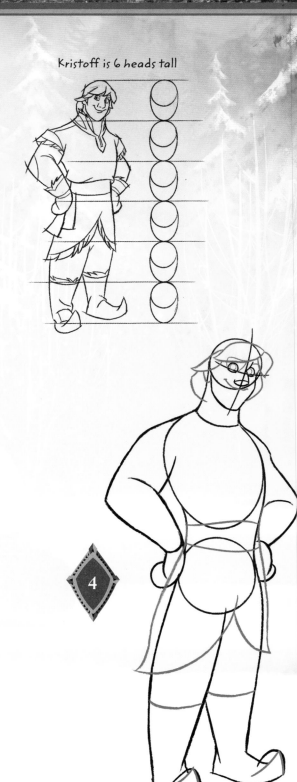

3

4

5

Kristoff's features follow these guidelines

1/3
1/2
1/2

Kristoff's eyes are
round, not angular

6

SVEN

Sven is Kristoff's loyal reindeer and constant companion, and the two have been inseparable since childhood. Sven is fiercely loyal to Kristoff and would do anything for his best friend. Although Sven doesn't speak, Kristoff knows exactly what Sven is thinking at all times—and he's not shy about giving his opinion! Sven loves carrots and is determined to take a bite out of Olaf's nose, if only the little snowman would hold still.

7

HANS

Hans is a handsome prince from a neighboring kingdom. With twelve older brothers, Hans grew up feeling practically invisible like Anna, and he promises that he'll never shut her out of his life the way Elsa has. Anna quickly falls head over heels for Hans, but she doesn't realize that Hans has a cold, conniving scheme, fueled by his hunger for admiration and power.

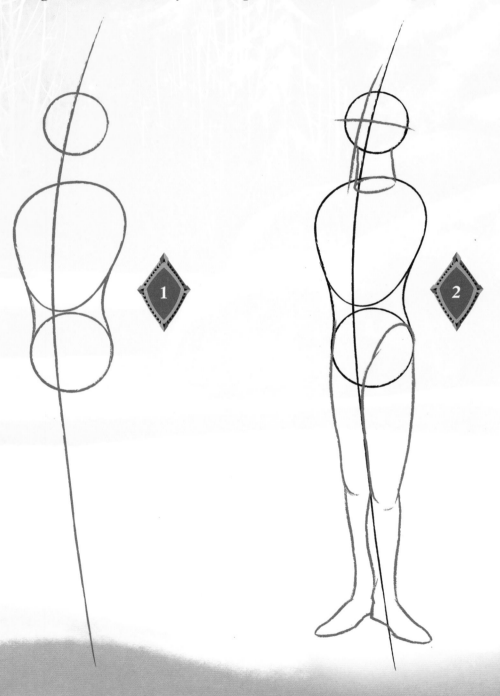

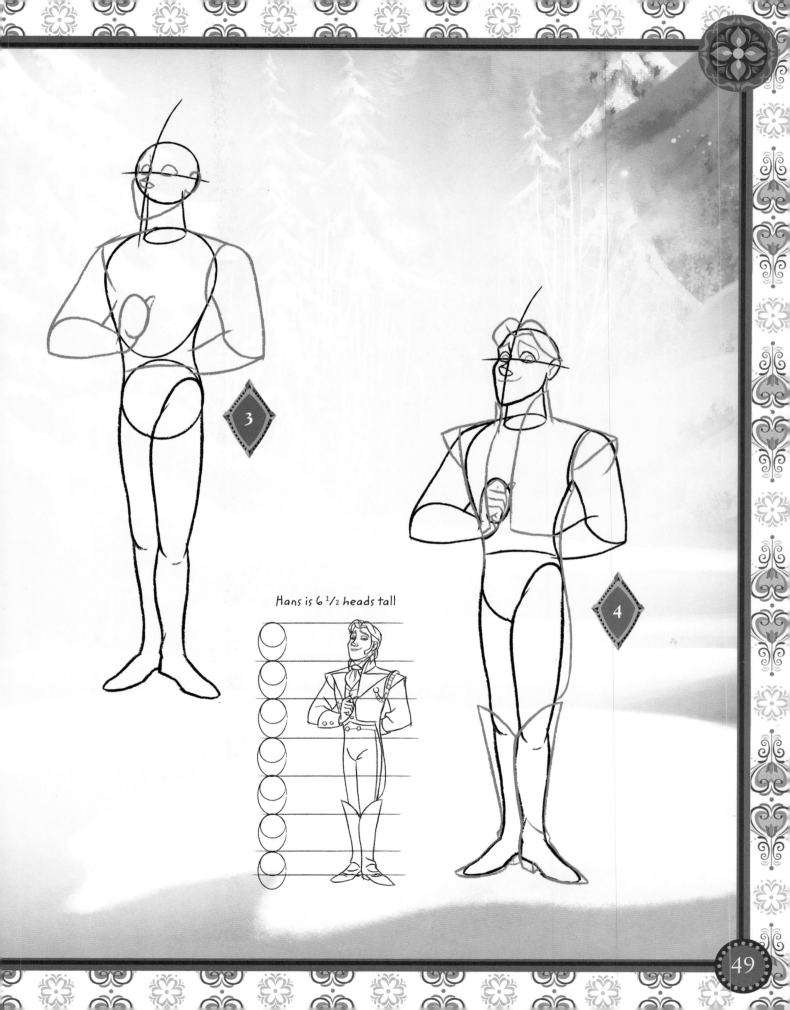

3

Hans is 6 ½ heads tall

4

Oval of nose is
tilted upward

Tip of nose is sharp
and angular

5

6

7

SITRON

Sitron is a Fjord horse, a native breed of Norway. He belongs to Prince Hans and accompanies him to Arendelle for Elsa's coronation. Sitron has a round, strong build and a black and cream colored mane.

By Maria

3

4

7

MARSHMALLOW

Marshmallow is the enormous snowman Elsa creates to protect her icy palace on the North Mountain. He serves as a brute bodyguard that doesn't say much but still packs a powerful punch.

3

4

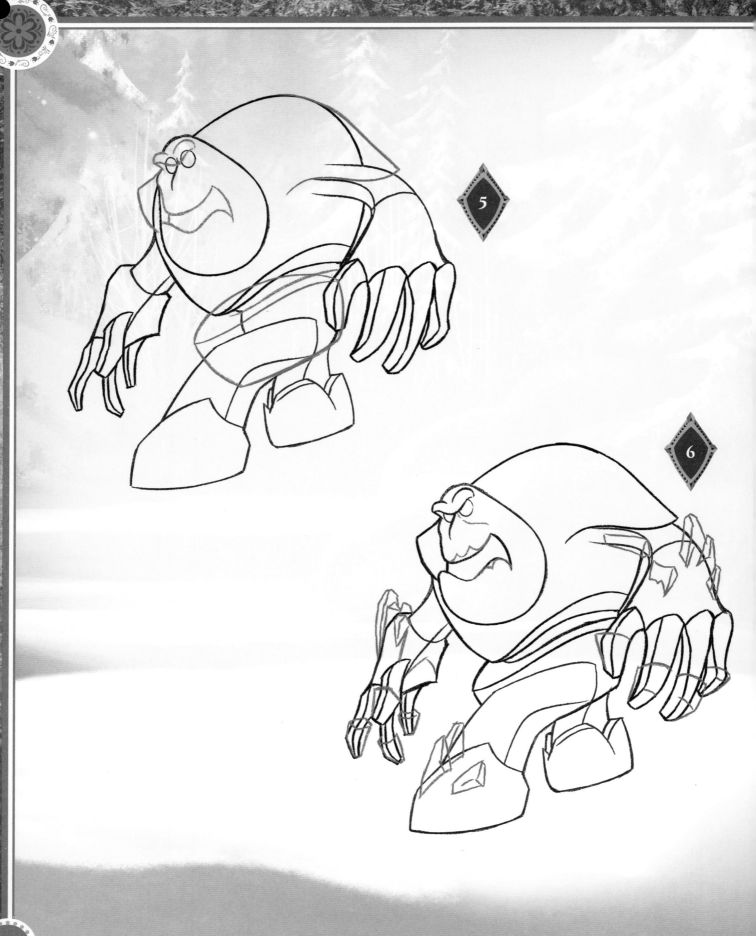

5

6

PABBIE

Pabbie is the wise and elderly ruler of the trolls and the mystical area known as the Valley of the Living Rock. When Kristoff was adopted by the troll community as a young boy, Pabbie took on the role of his grandfather, adopting the nickname "Grand Pabbie." He is a kind and gentle soul and is always willing to help those in need.

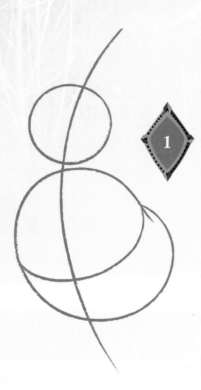

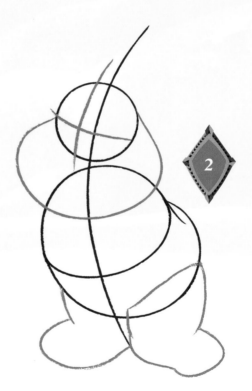

3

4

5

6

7

The End

Now that you've learned the secrets to
drawing your favorite characters from *Frozen,*
try creating different scenes from the movie.
With your pencil, paper, and a little imagination,
even the wildest of dreams can come true!